THE TALE OF TWO

AN OUTGOING AND AN INCOMING PRIME MINISTER

THE ONE WHO DID NOT SPEAK A WORD. HIS SILENCE WAS DEAFENING AND THE OTHER WHO SPOKE MUCH AND IT WAS DEAFENING. OUR GREAT MAHATMA WOULD HAVE SAID "HE SPOKE ENOUGH FOR BOTH OF US". BUT PERHAPS THE NATION WAS LONGING TO HEAR SOMETHING.

IT WAS AFTER 25 LONG YEARS, I FOUND THE COURAGE TO PHOTOGRAPH ONCE AGAIN THE SESSIONS OF TWO LEADING POLITICAL PARTIES DURING ELECTION SEASON, THE INDIAN NATIONAL CONGRESS AND BHARTIYA JANATA PARTY.

THOUGH IT WAS THE MONTH OF JANUARY, THE WEATHER OUTSIDE WAS PLEASANT. BUT DURING THOSE FOUR HOURS I SPENT INSIDE, THERE WAS A STRANGE KIND OF STUFFINESS IN THE ARENAS. STATISTICS TELL US, OVER 60% OF OUR POPULATION COMPRISES THE YOUNG – YOUTHFUL INDIA. HOW I LONGED FOR A BREATH OF REFRESHING YOUTHFUL ENERGY TO HELP ME UNDERSTAND THE PRESENT WITH AN EYE ON THE FUTURE OF A NATION ON THE MOVE. BUT A STRANGE KIND OF SYCOPHANCY AND PERSONALITY CULT ARE ENTRENCHED IN BOTH THE PARTIES; AS IF THE OTHER MEMBERS ARE LESSER BEINGS WHO SEEM ENTIRELY ACCEPTING OF THEIR LOWLY STATUS.

AICC

NG
READY

युवाकाँग्रेस
YOUTH CONGRESS

Chandra
Kripalani
Sitaramayya
(1948, 1949)

10:25 am

10:27 am

10:34 am

OUTGOING PRIME MINISTER MANMOHAN SINGH HOPES HISTORY WILL JUDGE HIM KINDLY. IT IS MY UNDERSTANDING THAT WHEN THE SUPREME POWER BRINGS A WAVE TO TAKE YOU UP AND GRANT YOU THE OPPORTUNITY TO BE THE SUPREME COMMANDER OF A NATION AS LARGE AND AS COMPLEX AS INDIA, IT ALSO EXPECTS YOU TO PERFORM YOUR DUTY AS A TRUE AND INTUITIVE REPRESENTATIVE OF THIS FORCE. POLITICAL COMPULSIONS AND RELIGIOUS MANIPULATIONS CEASE TO HOLD ANY MEANING IN THE LARGER INTEREST OF A NATION AND OUR PART OF THE DUTY MUST BE PERFORMED BY EACH ONE OF US FLAWLESSLY. IN THIS, NOBODY GETS ANOTHER CHANCE, JUST LIKE MANMOHAN SINGH WOULD NOT GET A THIRD CHANCE.

MOST OF US AGREE THAT DURING THE 2009 ELECTIONS, MANMOHAN SINGH'S IMAGE WAS AN ASSET FOR THE CONGRESS. HE WAS PERCEIVED TO BE AN ABLE AND HARDWORKING PRIME MINISTER WHO MADE IT POSSIBLE FOR THE CONGRESS PARTY TO COME TO POWER FOR A SECOND TERM. SOMEWHERE ALONG THE WAY THOUGH THINGS BEGAN GOING TERRIBLY WRONG WHICH WERE OVERLOOKED OR IGNORED BY HIM, AND HE SEEMED TO BE PLAGUED WITH INACTION WHEN IT CAME TO REMEDYING THEM. IT IS NOW MR. SINGH'S SILENCE OVER MAJOR ISSUES OF GOVERNANCE OR "RAJDHARMA" THAT HAS CAUSED AN UNPRECEDENTED DEFEAT FOR THE INDIAN NATIONAL CONGRESS, THE PARTY THAT FOUGHT FOR THE FREEDOM OF THIS NATION UNDER THE LEADERSHIP OF STALWARTS LIKE MAHATMA GANDHI, JAWAHARLAL NEHRU AND SARDAR PATEL.

THE PHOTOGRAPHS ON THE FOLLOWING PAGES WERE TAKEN ON 17 JANUARY 2014 BETWEEN 9:30 AM AND 1:30 PM. NEXT DAY WHEN I SAT AT MY COMPUTER TO EDIT IN THE BEST ONES, AS I WENT THROUGH THE IMAGES ONE BY ONE ON THE LARGE SCREEN, I WAS PAINED BY WHAT I SAW !

EARLIER ON I HAVE PHOTOGRAPHED AND EXPERIENCED IN VARIOUS POLITICAL SESSIONS OF LEADING PARTIES, RELATIONSHIPS, MANIPULATIONS, SYCOPHANCY AND POWER PLAY. BUT THE PRIME MINISTER OF THE DAY USED

TO BE THE FOCUS OF ATTENTION AND INTEREST AND EVERYONE IN THE PARTY LOOKED UP TO HIM FOR AN INTERACTION OR EVEN A SMILE.

IN MR. SINGH'S CASE, HE WALKS IN BEHIND SONIA GANDHI AT 10:30 AM, AND SITS A FEW FEET AWAY LOOKING LONELY AND ISOLATED. THERE IS ONLY A TINGE OF A RELUCTANT SMILE ON HIS FACE WHEN HE STANDS BETWEEN SONIA GANDHI AND RAHUL GANDHI SHARING A BIG GARLAND MEANT FOR THE TRIO.

EVERY MOMENT THAT I PHOTOGRAPHED HIM, THERE WAS THE SAME FIXED EXPRESSION OF GLOOM ON HIS FACE, AS IF HE WAS LIVING A NIGHTMARE. I WAS UNNERVED AND ASKED MYSELF "WHO HAS DONE THIS TO HIM AND WHY HAVE THEY DONE IT TO HIM OR HAS HE DONE IT TO HIMSELF".

THE OTHER SAD PART WAS, IN THOSE FEW HOURS THAT I WAS THERE AT THE CONGRESS SESSION, NOBODY CAME TO DISCUSS OR SHARE ANYTHING WITH HIM AS IF HE DID NOT MATTER ANY MORE. HE LOOKED ISOLATED, IGNORED AND DESERTED.

OF COURSE, EVERY NOW AND THEN, THERE WERE CHEERS AND 'JAI JAI KAAR' FOR RAHUL AND SONIA GANDHI, BUT NOBODY SHOWED ANY COURTESY TO THE TWO-TIME PRIME MINISTER WHO WAS ABOUT TO COMPLETE HIS TERM. I AM COMPELLED TO NARRATE THIS IN SIMPLE WORDS BUT I DO SO WITH A HEAVY HEART. SOME TRUTHS HAVE TO BE SHARED FOR FUTURE REFERENCE FOR THE NATION AS A WHOLE OR EVEN FOR THE POLITICAL PARTIES TO BE ABLE TO LOOK AT THEMSELVES ALL OVER AGAIN FROM AN HONEST AND SIMPLE HUMAN PERSPECTIVE.

ALAS! THE BIG GUYS IN POLITICAL POWER RARELY HAVE FRIENDS OR WELL-WISHERS WHO WOULD, REGARDLESS, SHARE THE INSTINCTIVE TRUTH IN ANY GIVEN SITUATION, POLITICAL, SOCIAL OR PERSONAL. ALL OF US, ESPECIALLY IN TESTING TIMES, PREFER TO LISTEN TO WHAT WOULD PLEASE OUR EARS. IN THE PROCESS, THE LARGER TRUTH IS THE CASUALTY AND YET THE RESULTS ARE UNACCEPTABLE.

10:36 am

10:37 am

10:38 am

भारतीय राष्ट्रीय कांग्रेस
INDIAN NATIONAL CONGRESS
अखिल भारतीय कांग्रेस कमेटी की बैठक
AICC Meeting
17 January, 2014
PRIME MINISTER

10:44 am

10:46 am

11:01 am

11:04 am

11:10 am

11:16 am

INDIAN NATIONAL
CONGRESS

11:18 am

11:20 am

11:24 am

11:46 am

11: 57 am

12:09 pm

12:12 pm

12:13 pm

12:14 pm

12:14 pm

2:56 pm

PHOTO : PTI

PHOTO : PTI

3:11 pm

PHOTO : PTI

4:25 pm

PROBABLY THIS WAS THE DETERMINATION BORN OUT OF TWO LOST OPPORTUNITIES DESPITE HAVING A GOVERNMENT AT THE CENTRE. BY AND LARGE WE HAVE SEEN A LACK OF CREDIBLE LEADERSHIP OF A NATIONAL STATURE IN THE TWO LEADING POLITICAL PARTIES OF THE COUNTRY. THEN THERE WAS SUDDENLY MODI AND ONLY MODI, NARENDRA MODI, BEING PROJECTED AS BJP/NDA'S FUTURE PRIME MINISTERIAL CANDIDATE. THE HEARTBURN AND ANGUISH WITHIN BJP AND OTHER REGIONAL PARTIES AS WELL AS THE RULING CONGRESS WERE ENORMOUS. AND THE CROSS-CURRENTS THREW UP MANY ISSUES, POLITICAL, SOCIAL, ESPECIALLY RELIGIOUS, AND SOMETIMES PERSONAL.

A BITTER ELECTION CAMPAIGN CONTINUED THROUGH THE BEGINNING OF MARCH TO THE MIDDLE OF MAY. A CAMPAIGN THAT SEEMED TO GO ON FOREVER, CAUSING THE EXCHEQUER THE LARGEST SUM OF MONEY EVER TO BE SPENT ON GENERAL ELECTIONS.

I WAS AT THE BHARTIYA JANATA PARTY'S NATIONAL COUNCIL MEETING AT RAMLILA GROUND ON 19 JANUARY FROM 9:30 AM TO 1:30 PM. ALL THE SENIOR LEADERS OF BJP WERE PRESIDING UNDER LARGER-THAN-LIFE HEADSHOTS OF NARENDRA MODI WHICH FORMED THE BACKDROP OF THE MAIN STAGE. SENIOR LEADERS LIKE ARUN JAITLEY, SUSHMA SWARAJ, VENKAIAH NAIDU, LOOKING TENSE AND SERIOUS, WERE ON THE LEFT SIDE OF THE STAGE AND ON THE RIGHT SIDE WERE THE WINNING STATE CHIEF MINISTERS LIKE RAMAN SINGH, SHIVRAJ CHAUHAN AND VASUNDHARA RAJE. NARENDRA MODI WAS AT THE CENTRE OF IT ALL. THEN ARRIVED THE SENIORMOST LEADER, THE ANNOYED ELDER SON OF THE FAMILY, L. K. ADVANI. THERE WAS A LITTLE FLUTTER, RESERVED GREETINGS WERE EXCHANGED.

EACH OF THESE LEADERS GOT UP TO SPEAK, MODI'S IMAGE LOOKING OUT OVER THEIR HEADS. IT WAS CLEAR THAT MODI WAS TO BE THE PROJECTION OF THE DAY.

THEN NARENDRA MODI STOOD UP TO SPEAK. A NEWLY PROGRAMMED,

WELL-DESIGNED, WELL- WORDED CAMPAIGN DECLAMATION CAME POURING OUT OF HIM WITH PROPER EMOTIONAL PUNCTUATIONS. THE AUDIENCE LISTENED SPELLBOUND. HE PROJECTED HIMSELF AS A COMPREHENSIVE AND WELL-AWARE LEADER OF A PARTY THAT WAS MISSING EVER SINCE MR. VAJPAYEE WITHDREW FROM ACTIVE POLITICAL LIFE. AFTER THE 2002 GUJARAT RIOTS, IT WAS MR. VAJPAYEE WHO HAD CAUTIONED MODI AND TALKED ABOUT "RAJDHARMA".

NOW THAT HE TAKES OVER AS THE NEW PRIME MINISTER, APART FROM HIS HARDCORE CRITICS, MANY IN INDIA HAVE GREAT HOPES OF HIM TAKING THE COUNTRY TOWARDS GOOD GOVERNANCE. GOOD GOVERNANCE WHERE EVERY SECTION OF SOCIETY REGARDLESS OF THEIR RELIGIOUS AFFILIATION SHALL HAVE AN EQUAL AND JUST OPPORTUNITY TO MAKE A DIFFERENCE TO THEIR OWN LIVES AS WELL AS THE COMMUNITY AND THE COUNTRY AT LARGE. GOOD GOVERNANCE WHERE WE HOPE TO HAVE CORRUPTION-FREE SYSTEMS IN PLACE BECAUSE PEOPLE HAVEN'T FORGOTTEN THE YEDYURAPPAS OF THE BJP ALSO.

SINCE A PRIME MINISTER IS THE SUPREME LEADER OF A NATION THERE IS NO ROOM FOR US TO LOOK FOR THE DETRACTORS WHO MIGHT HAVE BEEN THE CAUSE OF HIS FAILURE. IN MANMOHAN SINGH'S CASE HIS FAILURE TO GIVE US THE KIND OF GOVERNMENT WE WANTED MIGHT HAVE BEEN BECAUSE OF THE HIGH COMMAND'S FINAL DECISION OR THE SCAMS CAUSED BY THE RAJAS AND KALMADIS OF THE RULING UPA, BUT THE SOLE RESPONSIBILITY FALLS UPON THE PRIME MINISTER OF THE DAY. SIMILARLY WHEN NARENDRA MODI TAKES OVER, HIS PERFORMANCE AS PM WILL HAVE TO BE JUDGED BY HIS ACTIONS AND DECISIONS IN PERFORMING HIS "RAJDHARMA". YOU MAY CALL IT RESPONSIBILITY OR LIABILITY. BUT IF THINGS START GOING WRONG AGAIN, THEN HE TOO SHOULD NOT GO BLAMING HIS HIGH COMMAND RSS FOR HAVING UNDERMINED THE STRENGTH AND STATURE OF A PRIME MINISTER.

MODI FOR PM
MODI FO
भाजपा ही विकल्प

MODI FOR PM

KAMAL
DELHI
KAMAL SOUND
M-98111-39440 NEW DELH

KAMAL SOUND
M-98111-39440 NEW DELHI

Bharatiy
राष्ट्री
Natio

ya Janata Party
ीय परिषद्
nal Council
, दिल्ली

राष्ट्रीय परिषद्

Bharatiya

Prime Minister designate Narendra Modi being congratulated by BJP parliamentary board members at Parliament house, 17th May 2014

OUR PRIME MINISTER

PRIME MINISTER DESIGNATE NARENDRA MODI AFTER BEING DESIGNATED BOWED AND KISSED THE FLOOR OF PARLIAMENT HOUSE. HE SPOKE FROM THE HEART WITHOUT CRITICIZING THE PREVIOUS GOVERNMENT, HE TALKED ABOUT THE PURITY OF HEART AND HONESTY OF ACTION IN THE TEMPLE OF DEMOCRACY.

WE THE PEOPLE OF INDIA ARE

HAS PROMISED....

"WE ARE HERE IN THE TEMPLE OF DEMOCRACY. WE WILL WORK WITH ALL PURITY... NOT FOR THE POST BUT THE PEOPLE OF THE COUNTRY. WORK AND RESPONSIBILITY ARE THE BIGGEST THINGS."

"VARIOUS GOVERNMENTS IN THE PAST TRIED TO DO SOME GOOD WORK IN THEIR OWN WAY FOR WHICH THEY DESERVE APPRECIATION. WHATEVER GOOD HAS HAPPENED, WE WILL CARRY IT FORWARD."

"A GOVERNMENT IS ONE WHICH THINKS ABOUT THE POOR, LISTENS TO THE POOR AND WHICH EXISTS FOR THE POOR. THEREFORE, THE NEW GOVERNMENT IS DEDICATED TO THE POOR."

"MILLIONS OF YOUTH AND MOTHERS AND DAUGHTERS WHO ARE STRIVING FOR THEIR RESPECT AND HONOUR. VILLAGERS, FARMERS, DALITS AND THE OPPRESSED, THIS GOVERNMENT IS FOR THEM, FOR THEIR ASPIRATIONS AND THIS IS OUR RESPONSIBILITY. AND THIS IS OUR RESPONSIBILITY."

"WE WERE NOT FORTUNATE TO HAVE DIED FOR THE COUNTRY, BUT FOR EVERY CITIZEN BORN IN INDEPENDENT INDIA, HE SHOULD DEDICATE HIMSELF TO LIVE FOR THE COUNTRY. EVERY MOMENT OF OUR LIVES AND EVERY SPECK OF OUR BODY SHOULD BE DEDICATED TO 125 CRORE PEOPLE OF THIS COUNTRY, WE HAVE TO CARRY THIS DREAM. THE COUNTRY WILL THEN PROGRESS RAPIDLY."

"WHO SAYS CORRUPTION IS NECESSARY? MERA MANTRA HAI, NA KHATA HUN, NA KHANE DUNGA"
(MY MANTRA IS NEITHER DO I INDULGE IN CORRUPTION, NOR ALLOW ANYBODY ELSE)

THERE WILL BE "LESS GOVERNMENT AND MORE GOVERNANCE"
"AN ERA OF RESPONSIBILITY HAS BEGUN. IN 2019, I WILL MEET ALL OF YOU AGAIN WITH A REPORT CARD."

WAITING AND WATCHING....

First published in India in 2014 by:
Raghu Rai
Raghu Rai Center For Photography
raghuraicenterforphotography.com

ISBN: 978-81-928551-6-5

Book design : Raghu Rai
Technical support : Amit Chauhan

Printed and bound at
Lustra Print Process Pvt Ltd
New Delhi

Publishing facilitation: AuthorsUpFront
Distribution: FEEL Books